fast & fun lap quilts

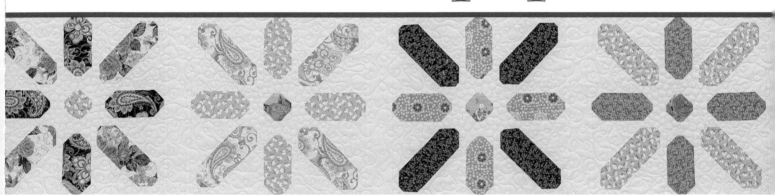

9 PATTERNS for 10" SQUARES

Melissa Corry

C&T PUBLISHING
Another Maker Inspired!

Copyright © 2022 by Melissa Corry
Publisher: Amy Barrett-Daffin
Creative Director: Gailen Runge
Senior Editor: Roxane Cerda
Technical Editor: Nancy Mahoney
Copy Editor: Durby Peterson
Illustrator: Sandy Loi
Book Designer: Angie Haupert Hoogensen
Photographer: Brent Kane
Production Coordinator: Zinnia Heinzmann

Published by C&T Publishing, Inc., P.O. Box 1456, Lafayette, CA 94549

Attention Teachers: C&T Publishing, Inc., encourages the use of our books as texts for teaching. You can find lesson plans for many of our titles at ctpub.com or contact us at ctinfo@ctpub.com.

We take great care to ensure that the information included in our products is accurate and presented in good faith, but no warranty is provided, nor are results guaranteed. Having no control over the choices of materials or procedures used, neither the author nor C&T Publishing, Inc., shall have any liability to any person or entity with respect to any loss or damage caused directly or indirectly by the information contained in this book. For your convenience, we post an up-to-date listing of corrections on our website (ctpub.com). If a correction is not already noted, please contact our customer service department at ctinfo@ctpub.com or P.O. Box 1456, Lafayette, CA 94549.

Trademark (™) and registered trademark (®) names are used throughout this book. Rather than use the symbols with every occurrence of a trademark or registered trademark name, we are using the names only in the editorial fashion and to the benefit of the owner, with no intention of infringement.

Library of Congress Control Number: 2023932131

Printed in the USA
10 9 8 7 6 5 4 3 2

DEDICATION

To my family

contents

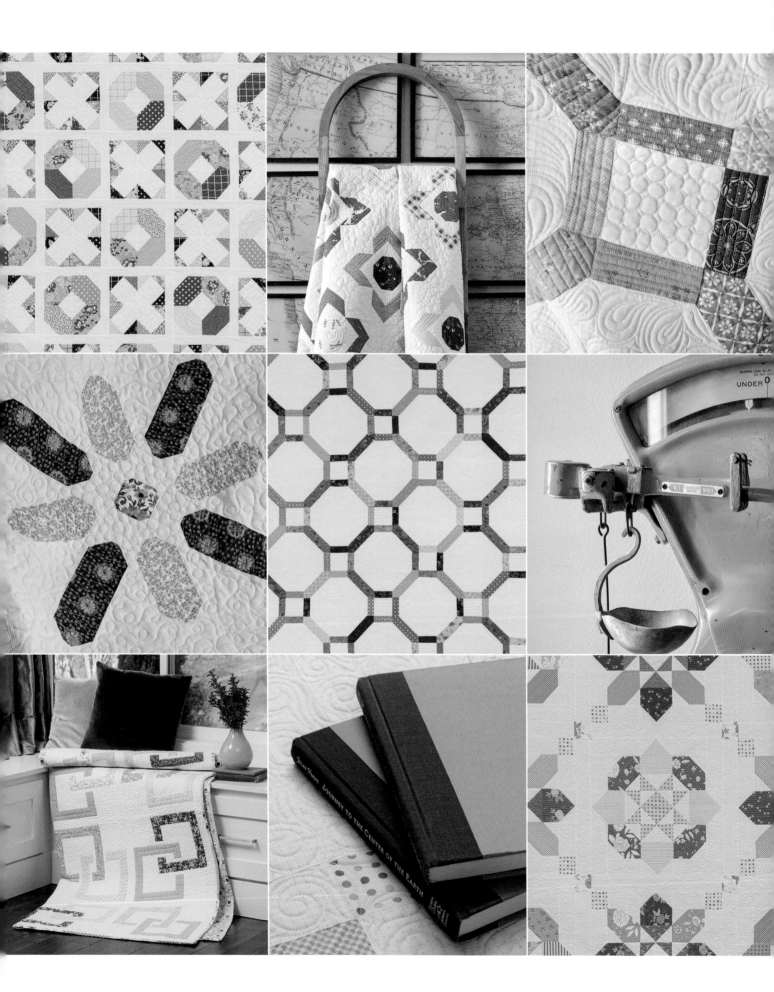

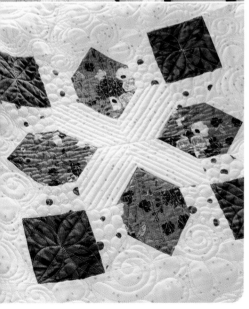

introduction

I have always loved working with precuts. It's so great to have a perfect combination of colors and prints all picked out and just waiting to be sewn into something amazing. And I'll admit, I have lots and lots of precuts stacked up in my sewing room.

In 2020, I wrote a book of baby quilt designs all made from charm packs. It was so much fun to transform all of those amazing 5" squares into quilts that would be cherished. So that got me thinking, why not do the same thing with 10" squares? And that led to *Fast & Fun Lap Quilts.*

All of the quilts in this book are geared to show off just how much you can get out of one Layer Cake. (A Moda Fabrics Layer Cake contains 42 squares, 10" × 10". Other fabric companies also offer precut 10" squares, but check the labels before you buy so you know exactly how many squares you'll have.) I know we all hate fabric waste, so when I say each quilt uses one bundle of 10" squares, it really does use pretty much the entire bundle.

No simple stack blocks here—each pattern shows off an amazing design that may look complex but is actually super simple when broken down into basic units. That's what makes all these quilts perfect for beginners and experts alike.

Lap quilts make wonderful gifts. They're ideal for a wedding, anniversary, retirement celebration, or just to show someone you love them. They're the perfect size for a treasured one to snuggle up in and enjoy. And I'm thrilled that you can whip up each of these lap quilts with just one Layer Cake plus a background fabric. Grab a Layer Cake from your stash or from your favorite quilt shop and get cutting and stitching in no time.

I hope you enjoy making these lovable lap quilts. Happy quilting!

~Melissa

three in a row

Often, while out to dinner with my family, I'll see something that inspires a quilt idea. I'll sketch it on my paper napkin using crayons that are on the table for the kids. It never fails—right after I finish my sketch, my daughter will promptly draw a tic-tac-toe board on that same napkin and want me to play. So I figured, why not use *that* for the inspiration behind a design? And that's how Three in a Row came to be.

materials

Yardage is based on 42"-wide fabric. A Moda Fabrics Layer Cake contains 42 squares, 10" × 10". Fabrics are One Fine Day by Bonnie and Camille for Moda Fabrics.

35 squares, 10" × 10", of assorted prints for blocks

3¼ yards of white solid for blocks and sashing

⅝ yard of navy dot for binding

3½ yards of fabric for backing

61" × 71" piece of batting

PLAN AHEAD

Divide the 10" squares into two groups as follows, and keep the fabrics labeled while making the blocks to achieve the desired results.

✳ *GROUP A: 20 assorted squares for X blocks*

✳ *GROUP B: 15 assorted squares for O blocks*

cutting

All measurements include ¼" seam allowances. Before you begin cutting, see "Plan Ahead," below left.

From *each* of the A squares, cut:
9 squares, 2¾" × 2¾" (180 total)

From *each* of the B squares, cut:
4 squares, 5" × 5" (60 total)

From the white solid, cut:
8 strips, 5" × 42"; crosscut into 60 squares, 5" × 5"
9 strips, 2¾" × 42"; crosscut into 120 squares, 2¾" × 2¾"
19 strips, 2" × 42"; crosscut *9 of the strips* into 36 strips, 2" × 9½"

From the navy dot, cut:
7 strips, 2½" × 42"

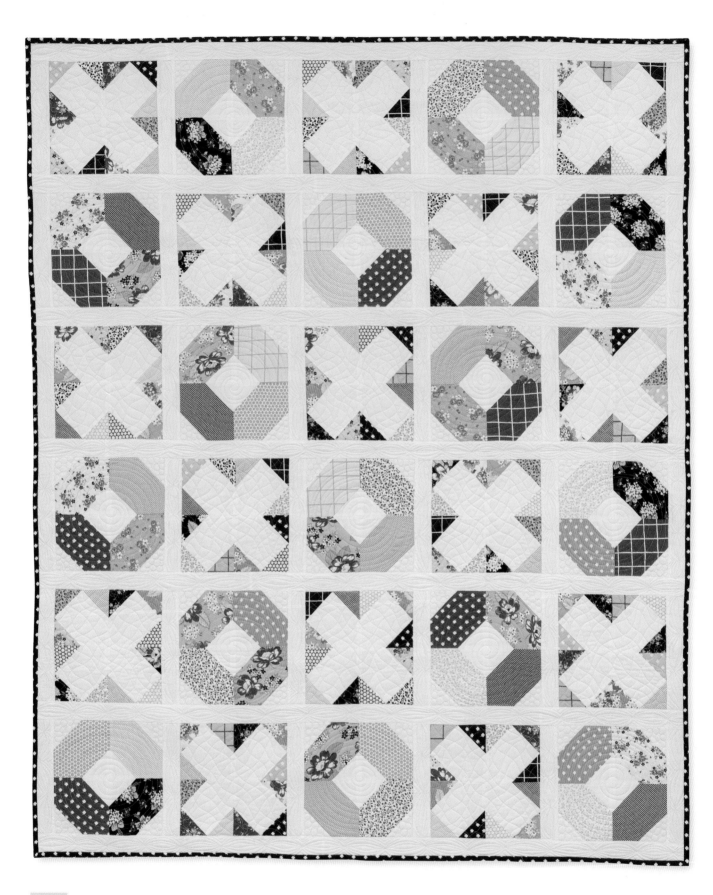

FINISHED QUILT: 54½" × 65"
FINISHED BLOCKS: 9" × 9"

making the X blocks

Press seam allowances in the directions indicated by the arrows.

1 Draw a diagonal line from corner to corner on the wrong side of the A squares. Place marked squares on opposite corners of a white 5" square, right sides together. Sew on the marked lines. Trim the excess corner fabric ¼" from the stitched lines. Place a marked square on the upper-left corner of the white square. If you want to avoid drawing lines, see "Skip Drawing Lines" on page 28. Sew and trim as before to make an A unit. Make 60 units measuring 5" square, including seam allowances.

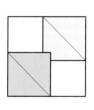 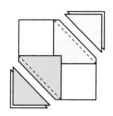

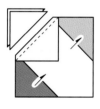

Make 60 A units,
5" × 5".

2 Lay out four A units in two rows, rotating the units as shown to form a white X. Sew the units into rows and then join the rows to make a block. Make 15 X blocks measuring 9½" square, including seam allowances.

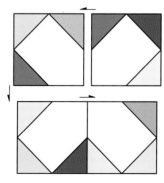

Make 15 X blocks,
9½" × 9½".

PRESSING MATTERS

Pressing the units as indicated will allow you to nest the diagonal seams, which makes aligning the points so much easier! When pressing the seam allowances in the same direction within a unit, press the unit from the right side. Place the unit on your ironing board, with the seam allowances pointing away from you. Press the new triangle away from yourself. When laying out the blocks, take care to position the pressed seam allowances in opposite directions from one block to the next, so the seams nest.

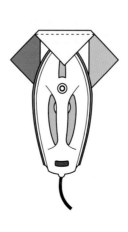 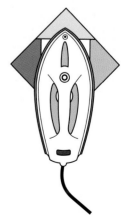

making the O blocks

1 Draw a diagonal line from corner to corner on the wrong side of the white 2¾" squares. Place marked squares on opposite corners of a B square, right sides together. Sew on the marked lines. Trim the excess corner fabric ¼" from the stitched lines. Make 60 B units measuring 5" square, including seam allowances.

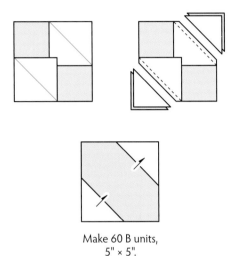

Make 60 B units,
5" × 5".

2 Lay out four B units in two rows, rotating them as shown to form an O. Sew the units into rows and then join the rows to make a block. Make 15 O blocks measuring 9½" square, including seam allowances.

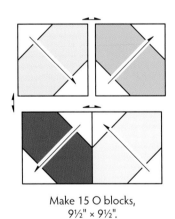

Make 15 O blocks,
9½" × 9½".

BONUS UNITS

You can easily make a bonus pillow or wall hanging from your scraps. Rather than throwing away the tiny triangles that you trim from the units, stitch a second line ½" from the first one. Cut between the stitched lines and trim each bonus half-square-triangle unit to 2" square. Sew the units in 17 rows of 17 units each. Join the rows to make a 26" square pillow or quilt top. It's so great to use every scrap!

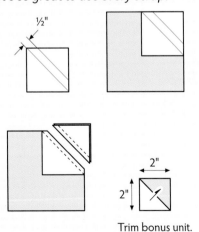

Trim bonus unit.

assembling the quilt top

1 Referring to the quilt assembly diagram below, join three X blocks, two O blocks, and six white 2" × 9½" strips to make an A row. Make three A rows measuring 9½" × 54½", including seam allowances.

2 Join three O blocks, two X blocks, and six white 2" × 9½" strips to make a B row. Make three B rows measuring 9½" × 54½", including seam allowances.

3 Join the white 2" × 42" strips end to end. From the pieced strip, cut seven 54½"-long sashing strips.

4 Join the 54½"-long sashing strips and block rows, alternating the A and B rows as shown. The quilt top should measure 54½" × 65".

finishing the quilt

1 Stitch around the perimeter of the quilt top, ⅛" from the outer edges, to lock the seams in place.

2 Layer the quilt top with batting and backing; baste the layers together.

3 Quilt by hand or machine. The quilt shown is machine quilted with swirls, pebbles, and wavy crosshatching in the blocks. Curved lines are stitched in the sashing.

4 Use the navy 2½"-wide strips to make double-fold binding. Attach the binding to the quilt.

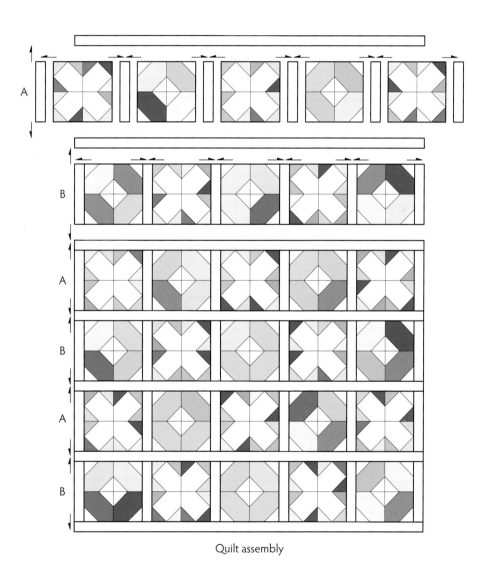

Quilt assembly

keystone corners

Inspiration truly comes from everywhere. This beauty was inspired by a garden path at a flower nursery, which had an amazing stonework design. I quickly snapped a picture, thinking it would be a wonderful quilt. And yes, I snap pictures of everything, including bathroom tiles! Keystone Corners is made with two simple units, so it's quick to piece. And it can also easily have a more masculine feel, depending on your fabric choices.

materials

Yardage is based on 42"-wide fabric. A Moda Fabrics Layer Cake contains 42 squares, 10" × 10". Fabrics are Meander by Aneela Hoey for Moda Fabrics.

35 squares, 10" × 10", of assorted prints for blocks

3¼ yards of white solid for blocks and sashing

⅝ yard of navy print for binding

3¾ yards of fabric for backing

67" × 67" piece of batting

PLAN AHEAD

The group A fabrics are used for the centers of each block, so they become the focal point of the quilt. I recommend using large-scale or novelty prints for the A squares.

Divide the 10" squares into two groups as follows, and keep the fabrics labeled while making the blocks to achieve the desired results.

* *GROUP A: 7 assorted squares for Snowball blocks*

* *GROUP B: 28 assorted squares for Arrow blocks*

cutting

All measurements include ¼" seam allowances. Before you begin cutting, see "Plan Ahead," below left.

From *each* of the A squares, cut:
4 squares, 4½" × 4½" (28 total; 3 are extra)

From *each* of the B squares, refer to the diagram below to cut:
1 square, 5¼" × 5¼" (28 total)
4 squares, 2⅞" × 2⅞" (112 total)

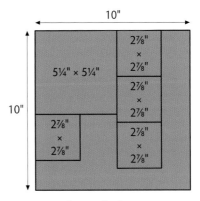

Cutting for B squares

From the white solid, cut:
4 strips, 5¼" × 42"; crosscut into 28 squares, 5¼" × 5¼"
11 strips, 4½" × 42"; crosscut into 88 squares, 4½" × 4½"
9 strips, 2⅞" × 42"; crosscut into 112 squares, 2⅞" × 2⅞"
5 strips, 1¾" × 42"; crosscut into 100 squares, 1¾" × 1¾"

From the navy print, cut:
7 strips, 2½" × 42"

FINISHED QUILT: 60½" × 60½"
FINISHED BLOCKS: 4" × 4"

If you find you really don't like cutting 2⅞" pieces, you can always upsize your pieces for the flying-geese units. Instead of 5¼" squares, cut 5½" squares and replace all of the 2⅞" squares with 3" squares. However, if you piece with these larger-size squares, you'll have to trim the units to 2½" × 4½" after piecing. I highly recommend using a flying-geese trimming ruler (such as a 2½" × 4½" Bloc Loc ruler) for trimming the units to size. Otherwise, it can be tricky to ensure that you maintain a ¼" seam allowance on all sides of the unit.

making the arrow blocks

Press seam allowances in the directions indicated by the arrows.

1 Draw a diagonal line from corner to corner on the wrong side of the B 2⅞" squares. Align two squares on opposite corners of a white 5¼" square, right sides together. The marked squares should overlap in the center. Sew ¼" from both sides of the drawn line. Cut the unit apart on the drawn line to make two units.

 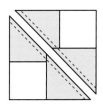

2 Place a marked square on the corner of the larger triangle of a unit from step 1, right sides together, noting the direction of the marked line. Sew ¼" from both sides of the drawn line. Cut the unit apart on the drawn line. Repeat with the remaining marked square and unit from step 1 to yield four flying-geese units. Trim the tails on the units. Make 28 sets of four matching units (112 total units) measuring 2½" × 4½", including seam allowances.

Make 28 sets of 4 matching units,
2½" × 4½".

3 Draw a diagonal line from corner to corner on the wrong side of the white 2⅞" squares. Repeat steps 1 and 2 using the B 5¼" squares and the marked squares to make 28 sets of four matching flying-geese units (112 total units).

Make 28 sets of 4 matching units,
2½" × 4½".

4 Join a step 3 unit to the top of a matching step 2 unit to make a block. Make 112 Arrow blocks measuring 4½" square, including seam allowances.

Make 112 Arrow blocks,
4½" × 4½".

Pressing the seam allowances open on the Arrow blocks will create a small V in the seam allowances along the outer edges. When sewing the units together, sew with the Arrow block on top so you can stitch right along the bottom point of the V, ensuring a perfect point on flying-geese units.

making the snowball blocks

Draw a diagonal line from corner to corner on the wrong side of the white 1¾" squares. Place marked squares on each corner of an A square, right sides together. Sew on the marked lines, then trim the excess corner fabric ¼" from the stitched lines. Make 25 Snowball blocks that measure 4½" square, including seam allowances.

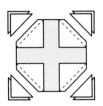

Make 25 Snowball blocks,
4½" × 4½".

assembling the quilt top

Referring to the quilt assembly diagram, lay out the blocks and white 4½" squares in 15 rows, placing four matching Arrow blocks around each Snowball block as shown. Sew the blocks and squares into rows and then join the rows. The quilt top should measure 60½" square.

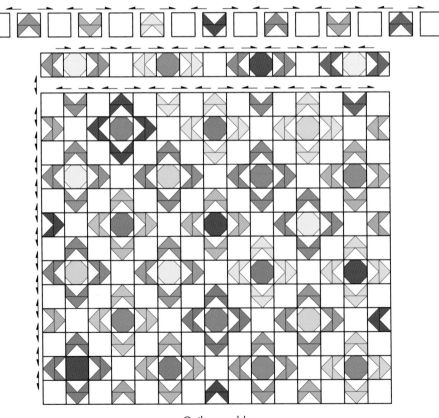

Quilt assembly

KEEPING THE ROWS SORTED

If you don't have a design wall, simply lay out the blocks on the floor. (I prefer carpet as it's softer on my knees.) Once the blocks are all laid out, mark the first block in each row with the row number. You can use numbered clothespins, fancy pins with numbers on them, or even a sticky note pinned to the square.

When piecing the rows, I like to chain piece two rows at a time. This saves time and thread, and also keeps me from accidentally mixing up any blocks, which happens whenever I try and sew more than two rows at a time.

After pressing, use the row markers to return the rows to their correct position in the layout to prevent mix-ups.

finishing the quilt

1 Stitch around the perimeter of the quilt top, ⅛" from the outer edges, to lock the seams in place.

2 Layer the quilt top with batting and backing; baste the layers together.

3 Quilt by hand or machine. The quilt shown is machine quilted with echoed arches and large spirals in the blocks. Loops and cobblestones are stitched in the background.

4 Use the navy 2½"-wide strips to make double-fold binding. Attach the binding to the quilt.

diamond dash

I love adding a twist to traditional quilt blocks to make them a little more modern. Here, I started with the classic Churn Dash block and created some diamond fun in the center. After designing that block, I knew a complementary block would echo the diamond center and produce a secondary pattern. Diamond Dash is fun and fast, a great quilt for anyone.

materials

Yardage is based on 42"-wide fabric. A Moda Fabrics Layer Cake contains 42 squares, 10" × 10". Fabrics are Seashore Drive by Sherri and Chelsi for Moda Fabrics.

38 squares, 10" × 10", of assorted prints for blocks and binding

3¾ yards of white solid for blocks and border

4 yards of fabric for backing

71" × 71" piece of batting

PLAN AHEAD

Divide the 10" squares into three groups as follows, and keep the fabrics labeled while making the blocks to achieve the desired results.

✱ *GROUP A: 13 assorted squares for Churn Dash block sides and binding*

✱ *GROUP B: 13 assorted squares for Churn Dash block corners and centers*

✱ *GROUP C: 12 assorted squares for Diamond blocks and binding*

cutting

All measurements include ¼" seam allowances. Before you begin cutting, see "Plan Ahead," below left.

From *each* of the A squares, cut:
1 strip, 2½" × 10" (13 total)
4 strips, 2" × 6½" (52 total)
2 squares, 2" × 2" (26 total; 2 are extra)

From *each* of the B squares, cut:
4 squares, 4" × 4" (52 total)
2 squares, 2" × 2" (26 total; 2 are extra)

From *each* of the C squares, cut:
2 squares, 5" × 5" (24 total)
2 strips, 2½" × 10" (24 total; 5 are extra)

From the white solid, cut:
5 strips, 8" × 42"; crosscut into 24 squares, 8" × 8". Cut the squares in half diagonally to yield 48 triangles.
3 strips, 5" × 42"; crosscut into 24 squares, 5" × 5"
6 strips, 4" × 42"; crosscut into 52 squares, 4" × 4"
7 strips, 2½" × 42"
12 strips, 2" × 42"; crosscut into:
     52 strips, 2" × 6½"
     52 squares, 2" × 2"

FINISHED QUILT: 64½" × 64½"
FINISHED BLOCKS: 12" × 12"

making the churn dash blocks

Press seam allowances in the directions indicated by the arrows.

1 Join one A 2" × 6½" strip and one white 2" × 6½" strip to make a side unit. Make 13 sets of four matching side units measuring 3½" × 6½", including seam allowances.

Make 13 sets of 4 matching units, 3½" × 6½".

2 Draw a diagonal line from corner to corner on the wrong side of the white 4" squares. Layer a marked square on a B 4" square, right sides together. Sew ¼" from both sides of the drawn line. Cut the unit apart on the marked line to make two half-square-triangle units. Repeat to make 13 sets of eight matching half-square-triangle units and trim them to 3½" square, including seam allowances. *Note:* In each set, the seam allowances in four units are pressed in one direction and the seam allowances in the other four units are pressed in the opposite direction.

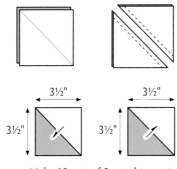

Make 13 sets of 8 matching units.

3 Draw a diagonal line from corner to corner on the wrong side of the white 2" squares. Place a marked square on the B corner of a half-square-triangle unit, right sides together. Sew on the marked line. Trim the excess corner fabric ¼" from the stitched line. Make 13 sets of four matching units measuring 3½" square,

including seam allowances. *Note:* In each set, press the seam allowances in each unit in the same direction as you did in step 2.

Make 13 sets of 4 matching units, 3½" × 3½".

4 Lay out four matching units from step 3 in two rows, rotating the units as shown. Sew the units into rows and then join the rows. Make 13 center units measuring 6½" square, including seam allowances.

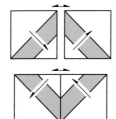 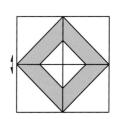

Make 13 units, 6½" × 6½".

NESTING ANGLED SEAMS

Take careful notice of the directions of the pressed seam allowances when laying out the units from step 3. Placing units next to each other with seam allowances that are pressed in opposite directions will allow you to nest the seams. Being able to nest the seams is a huge help when piecing the center units.

5 Lay out four matching half-square-triangle units, four matching side units, and one center unit in three rows as shown. Sew the units into rows and then join the rows. Make 13 Churn Dash blocks measuring 12½" square, including seam allowances.

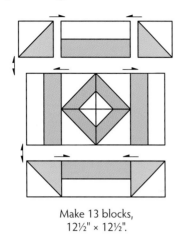

Make 13 blocks,
12½" × 12½".

making the diamond blocks

1 Draw a diagonal line from corner to corner on the wrong side of the white 5" squares. Layer a marked square on a C square, right sides together. Sew ¼" from both sides of the drawn line. Cut the unit apart on the marked line to make two half-square-triangle units. Repeat to make 12 sets of four matching units and trim them to 4½" square, including seam allowances. *Note:* In each set, the seam allowances in two units are pressed in one direction and the seam allowances in the other two units are pressed in the opposite direction.

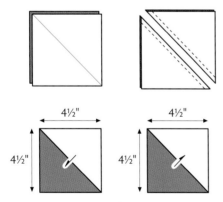

Make 12 sets of 4 matching units.

2 Draw a diagonal line from corner to corner on the wrong side of the A and B 2" squares. Place a marked square on the white corner of a half-square-triangle unit, right sides together. Sew on the marked line. Trim the excess corner fabric ¼" from the stitched line. Make 12 sets of four units with matching large

triangles, each measuring 4½" square, including seam allowances. *Note:* In each set, press the seam allowances in each unit in the same direction as you did in step 1.

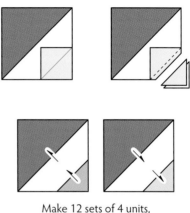

Make 12 sets of 4 units,
4½" × 4½".

3 Lay out four center units with matching outer triangles as shown to form a white diamond. Sew the units into rows and then join the rows. Make 12 center units measuring 8½" square, including seam allowances.

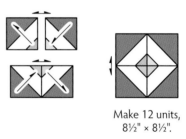

Make 12 units,
8½" × 8½".

4 Fold four white triangles in half and finger-press to mark the center of the long side. Sew triangles to opposite sides of a center unit, aligning the center crease and seamline. Trim the triangle tails even with the center unit. Sew triangles on the remaining sides of the unit. Make 12 Diamond blocks and trim them to 12½" square, including seam allowances. See "Keep It Centered" on page 23 for tips on trimming the blocks.

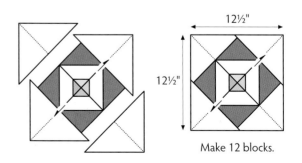

Make 12 blocks.

It's easy to square up your block and keep the center unit centered. To do so, place a 12½" square ruler on the Diamond block and align the 6¼" horizontal and vertical lines on your ruler with the seamlines of the center unit. Trim two sides. Rotate the block 180°, align the ruler, and trim the remaining two sides. You'll have a perfectly centered Diamond block, and the block is designed so the center will float. That means you'll have more than ¼" of white beyond the points. Don't worry—that's the way it should look.

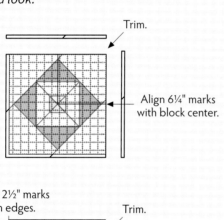

Trim.

Align 6¼" marks with block center.

Align 12½" marks with edges.

Trim.

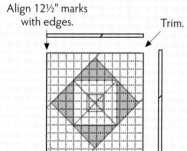

assembling the quilt top

1 Lay out the blocks in five rows of five blocks each, alternating the Churn Dash and Diamond blocks in each row and from row to row as shown on page 24. Sew the blocks into rows and then join the rows. The quilt top should measure 60½" square, including seam allowances.

2 Join the white 2½"-wide strips end to end. From the pieced strip, cut two 64½"-long strips and two 60½"-long strips. Sew the shorter strips to the left and right sides of the quilt top. Sew the longer strips to the top and bottom edges. The quilt top should measure 64½" square.

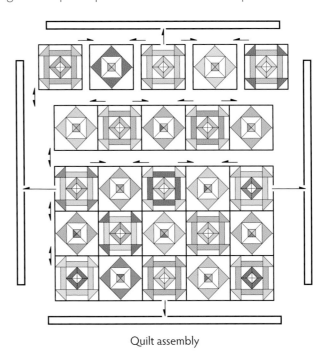

Quilt assembly

finishing the quilt

1 Layer the quilt top with batting and backing; baste the layers together.

2 Quilt by hand or machine. The quilt shown is machine quilted with echoed arches and ribbon candy in the blocks. Curlicues are stitched in the background.

3 Use the A and C 2½" × 10" strips to make scrappy double-fold binding. Attach the binding to the quilt.

SCRAPPY BINDINGS

A scrappy binding is a perfect way to finish a quilt that's made from lots of different fabrics. It sticks to the scrappy theme and it lets you use the leftovers from your quilt top. If you have never made a scrappy binding before, don't worry. It's the same as making a binding from one print, except you join a lot more strips and the strips are shorter.

aurora

I absolutely love designing Star blocks! Truly, they are my go-to bread and butter of designing. In Aurora, I added a pieced frame to a basic Ohio Star to create an amazing block. Then a simple change in the fabric placement and orientation made a wonderful new second block that forms a chain across the quilt top. The two blocks combine to make a stunning quilt.

materials

Yardage is based on 42"-wide fabric. A Moda Fabrics Layer Cake contains 42 squares, 10" × 10". Fabrics are Beautiful Day by Corey Yoder for Moda Fabrics.

33 squares, 10" × 10", of assorted prints for blocks

4⅛ yards of white solid for blocks and sashing

⅝ yard of gray print for binding

4⅛ yards of fabric for backing

74" × 74" piece of batting

PLAN AHEAD

Balancing the colors in this quilt is very important. Refer to the photo on page 32 and the block diagrams on pages 29 and 31 for placement guidance when selecting the fabrics for each group listed below. The fabrics in groups A–C will be used to make five O blocks. The fabrics in groups D–F will be used to make four X blocks. The fabrics in group G will be used for the sashing cornerstones. I recommend small-scale dark prints for the group F squares so the white stars in the X blocks stand out.

Divide the 10" squares into seven groups as follows, and keep the fabrics labeled while making the quilt to achieve the desired results.

❋ *GROUP A: 5 assorted squares for O block corners*

❋ *GROUP B: 5 assorted squares for O block sides*

❋ *GROUP C: 5 assorted squares for O block star centers*

❋ *GROUP D: 4 assorted squares for X block corners*

❋ *GROUP E: 4 assorted squares for X block sides*

❋ *GROUP F: 4 assorted squares for X block star centers*

❋ *GROUP G: 6 assorted squares for cornerstones*

cutting

All measurements include ¼" seam allowances. Before you begin cutting, see "Plan Ahead" on page 25.

From *each* of the A, B, D, and E squares, cut:
4 squares, 5" × 5" (72 total)

From *each* of the C squares, refer to the diagram to cut:
1 square, 5" × 5" (5 total)
4 squares, 3⅛" × 3⅛" (20 total)

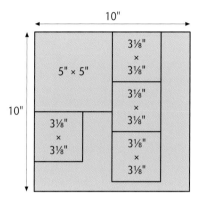

Cutting for C squares

From *each* of the F squares, refer to the diagram to cut:
1 square, 5¾" × 5¾" (4 total)
4 squares, 2¾" × 2¾" (16 total)

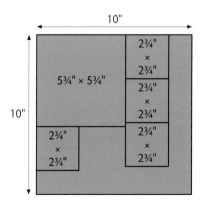

Cutting for F squares

From *each* of the G squares, cut:
8 squares, 2¾" × 2¾" (48 total)

From the white solid, cut:
1 strip, 5¾" × 42"; crosscut into 5 squares, 5¾" × 5¾"
1 strip, 5" × 42"; crosscut into 4 squares, 5" × 5"
2 strips, 3⅛" × 42"; crosscut into 16 squares, 3⅛" × 3⅛"
42 strips, 2¾" × 42"; crosscut into:
    4 strips, 2¾" × 23"
    24 strips, 2¾" × 18½"
    8 strips, 2¾" × 14"
    20 strips, 2¾" × 7¼"
    56 strips, 2¾" × 5"
    168 squares, 2¾" × 2¾"

From the gray print, cut:
8 strips, 2½" × 42"

making the O blocks

Press seam allowances in the directions indicated by the arrows.

1 Draw a diagonal line from corner to corner on the wrong side of 40 white 2¾" squares. Place marked squares on opposite corners of an A square, right sides together. Sew on the marked lines. Trim the excess corner fabric ¼" from the stitched lines. Make five sets of four matching units measuring 5" square, including seam allowances.

Make 5 sets of
4 matching units,
5" × 5".

USE EVERY SCRAP

If you don't like throwing away the tiny triangles trimmed from the stitch-and-flip units, use them to make bonus half-square-triangle units. Draw a second line ½" from the first one and then sew on both lines. Cut between the stitched lines and trim the bonus half-square-triangle unit to 2" square. Join the units in 13 rows of 13 units each to make a pillow top that measures 20" square, including seam allowances. The pillow top will be a perfect complement to your quilt.

2 Sew a white 2¾" × 5" strip to the left side of a unit from step 1. Join a white 2¾" × 7¼" strip to the top of the unit. Make five sets of four matching corner units measuring 7¼" square, including seam allowances.

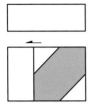
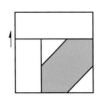

Make 5 sets of 4 matching units, 7¼" × 7¼".

3 Draw a diagonal line from corner to corner on the wrong side of 40 white 2¾" squares. Place a marked square on one corner of a B square, right sides together. Sew on the marked line. Trim the excess corner fabric ¼" from the stitched line. Place a marked square on an adjacent corner of the B square. Sew and trim as before. Make five sets of four matching units measuring 5" square, including seam allowances.

Make 5 sets of 4 matching units, 5" × 5".

SKIP DRAWING THE LINE

You can save time and avoid drawing lines by using any number of diagonal marking tools on your machine. My personal favorite is the Clearly Perfect Angles by New Leaf Stitches. I also love the Diagonal Seam Tape by Cluck Cluck Sew and the Seams Sew Easy seam guide by Lori Holt.

4 Draw a diagonal line from corner to corner on the wrong side of four matching C 3⅛" squares. Align two squares on opposite corners of a white 5¾" square, right sides together. The marked squares should overlap in the center. Sew ¼" from both sides of the drawn lines. Cut the unit apart on the drawn lines to make two units.

5 Place a marked square on the corner of the larger triangle in a unit from step 4, right sides together, noting the direction of the marked line. Sew ¼" from both sides of the drawn line. Cut the unit apart on the drawn line. Repeat with the remaining marked square and unit from step 4 to yield four flying-geese units measuring 2¾" × 5", including seam allowances. Repeat to make five sets of four matching units. Trim the tails from the units.

Make 5 sets of 4 matching units, 2¾" × 5".

6 Sew a flying-geese unit to the bottom of a unit from step 3 to make a side unit. Make five sets of four matching units measuring 5" × 7¼", including seam allowances.

Make 5 sets of 4 matching units, 5" × 7¼".

7 Draw a diagonal line from corner to corner on the wrong side of 20 white 2¾" squares. Place matching squares on opposite corners of a C 5" square, right sides together. Sew on the marked lines. Trim the excess corner fabric ¼" from the stitched lines. Place marked squares on the remaining corners of the square. Sew and trim as before to make a center unit. Make five units measuring 5" square, including seam allowances.

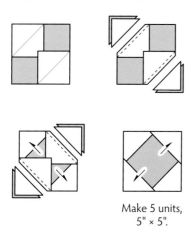

Make 5 units,
5" × 5".

8 Lay out four matching corner units, four matching side units, and one matching center unit in three rows as shown. Sew the units into rows and then join the rows to make an O block. Make five blocks measuring 18½" square, including seam allowances.

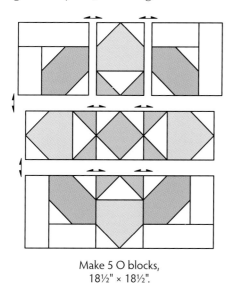

Make 5 O blocks,
18½" × 18½".

PERFECT POINTS

The blocks in this quilt have have lots of points to line up. Here's how to align the seams for perfect points:

Place two units right sides together, insert a pin through the back of the top unit, right at the triangle's tip. Separate the two units far enough to see the tip of the triangle on the bottom unit and push this positioning pin straight through that tip to establish the matching point.

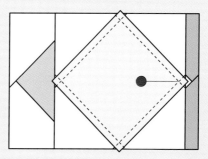

Pin through both layers of fabric on each side of the positioning pin; remove the positioning pin and pin the remainder of the seam.

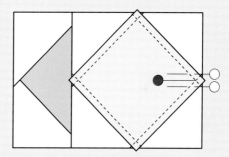

Stitch the seam so it's right along the bottom of the triangle tip. Check from the right side to make sure the points align. You may need to adjust the width of your seam allowance to achieve perfect points.

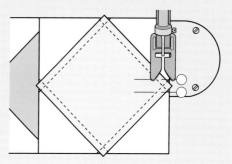

making the X blocks

1 Draw a diagonal line from corner to corner on the wrong side of 32 white 2¾" squares. Place marked squares on opposite corners of a D square, right sides together. Sew on the marked lines. Trim the excess corner fabric ¼" from the stitched lines. Make four sets of four matching units measuring 5" square.

Make 4 sets of
4 matching units,
5" × 5".

2 Join one unit from step 1, two white 2¾" × 5" strips, and one G 2¾" square to make a corner unit. Make four sets of four matching units measuring 7¼" square, including seam allowances.

Make 4 sets of 4 matching units,
7¼" × 7¼".

3 Draw a diagonal line from corner to corner on the wrong side of 32 white 2¾" squares. Place a marked square on one corner of an E square, right sides together. Sew on the marked line. Trim the excess corner fabric ¼" from the stitched line. Place a marked square on an adjacent corner of the E square. Sew and trim as before. Make four sets of four matching units measuring 5" square, including seam allowances.

Make 4 sets of 4 matching units,
5" × 5".

4 Draw a diagonal line from corner to corner on the wrong side of the white 3⅛" squares. Align two squares on opposite corners of an F 5¾" square, right sides together. The marked squares should overlap in the center. Sew ¼" from both sides of the drawn lines. Cut the unit apart on the drawn lines to make two units.

5 Place a marked square on the corner of the larger triangle of a unit from step 4, right sides together, noting the direction of the marked line. Sew ¼" from both sides of the drawn line. Cut the unit apart on the drawn line. Repeat with the remaining marked square and unit from step 4 to yield four flying-geese units measuring 2¾" × 5", including seam allowances. Repeat to make four sets of four matching units. Trim the tails from the units.

Make 4 sets of
4 matching units,
2¾" × 5".

6 Sew a flying-geese unit to the bottom of a unit from step 3 to make a side unit. Make four sets of four matching units measuring 5" × 7¼", including seam allowances.

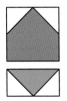

Make 4 sets of 4 matching units,
5" × 7¼".

7 Draw a diagonal line from corner to corner on the wrong side of the F 2¾" squares. Place matching squares on opposite corners of a white 5" square, right sides together. Sew on the marked lines. Trim the excess corner fabric ¼" from the stitched lines. Place matching marked squares on the remaining corners

FINISHED QUILT: 68" × 68"
FINISHED BLOCKS: 18" × 18"

of the square. Sew and trim as before to make a center unit. Make four units measuring 5" square, including seam allowances.

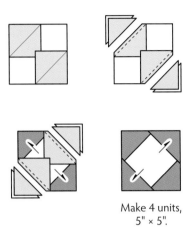

Make 4 units,
5" × 5".

8 Lay out four matching corner units, four matching side units, and one matching center unit in three rows as shown. Sew the units into rows and then join the rows. Make four X blocks measuring 18½" square, including seam allowances.

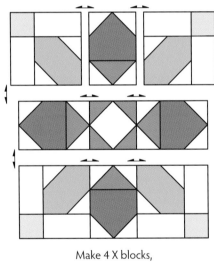

Make 4 X blocks,
18½" × 18½".

assembling the quilt top

Refer to the quilt assembly diagram on page 33 as needed throughout.

1 Join four G squares and three white 2¾" × 18½" strips to make a sashing row. Make four rows measuring 2¾" × 63½", including seam allowances.

2 Join three blocks and four white 2¾" × 18½" strips to make a block row. Make three rows measuring 18½" × 63½", including seam allowances.

3 Join the sashing rows alternately with the block rows. The quilt top should measure 63½" square, including seam allowances.

adding the borders

1 Join two white 2¾" squares, two white 2¾" × 14" strips, one white 2¾" × 23" strip, and four G 2¾" squares to make a side border measuring 2¾" × 63½", including seam allowances. Make two and sew them to the left and right edges of the quilt top.

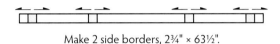

Make 2 side borders, 2¾" × 63½".

2 Join two white 2¾" × 5" pieces, two white 2¾" × 14" strips, one white 2¾" × 23" strip, and four G 2¾" squares to make a top border measuring 2¾" × 68", including seam allowances. Repeat to make the bottom border. Sew the borders to the top and bottom edges to complete the quilt top. The quilt top should measure 68" square.

Make 2 top/bottom borders, 2¾" × 68".

finishing the quilt

1 Layer the quilt top with batting and backing; baste the layers together.

2 Quilt by hand or machine. The quilt shown is machine quilted with straight lines and pebbles in the blocks. Swirls and arches are stitched in the background.

3 Use the gray 2½"-wide strips to make double-fold binding. Attach the binding to the quilt.

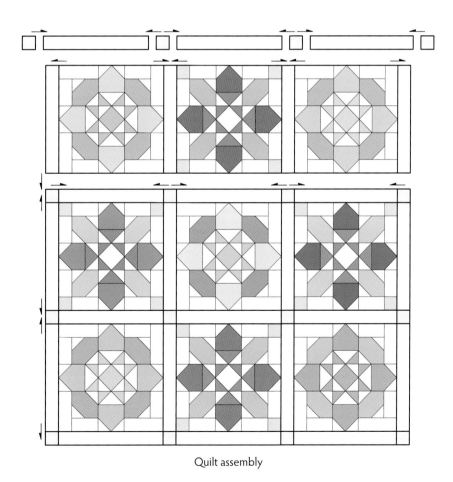

Quilt assembly

dutch days

Dutch Days reminds me of windmills blowing in large fields of tulips, which is how the quilt got its name. I purposely chose fabrics with colors reminiscent of tulip fields. Using the no-waste method for the flying-geese units makes this quilt super fast to piece, and mixing the prints in the units gives it a scrappy look without too much effort. It's a wonderful quilt to whip up for any special occasion.

materials

Yardage is based on 42"-wide fabric. A Riley Blake Designs 10" Stacker contains 42 squares, 10" × 10". Fabrics are Harmony by Melissa Lee for Riley Blake Designs.

40 squares, 10" × 10", of assorted prints for blocks

2⅞ yards of white solid for blocks and sashing

⅝ yard of plum print for binding

4⅜ yards of fabric for backing

78" × 78" piece of batting

PLAN AHEAD

Divide the 10" squares into two groups as follows, and keep the fabrics labeled while making the blocks to achieve the desired results.

* **GROUP A:** 24 assorted squares for blocks

* **GROUP B:** 16 assorted squares for blocks

cutting

All measurements include ¼" seam allowances. Before you begin cutting, see "Plan Ahead," above.

From *each* of the A squares, cut:
4 squares, 4⅞" × 4⅞" (96 total)

From *each* of the B squares, cut:
4 squares, 4½" × 4½" (64 total)

From the white solid, cut:
6 strips, 9¼" × 42"; crosscut into 24 squares, 9¼" × 9¼"
19 strips, 2" × 42"; crosscut *10 of the strips* into 20 strips, 2" × 16½"

From the plum print, cut:
8 strips, 2½" × 42"

making the dutch days blocks

Press seam allowances in the directions indicated by the arrows.

1 Draw a diagonal line from corner to corner on the wrong side of four assorted A squares. Align two squares on opposite corners of a white 9¼" square, right sides together. The marked squares should overlap in the center. Sew ¼" from both sides of the drawn lines. Cut the unit apart on the drawn lines to make two units.

 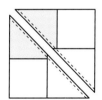

FINISHED QUILT: 72" × 72"
FINISHED BLOCKS: 16" × 16"

2 Place a marked square on the corner of the larger triangle of a unit from step 1, right sides together, noting the direction of the marked line. Sew ¼" from both sides of the drawn line. Cut the unit apart on the drawn line. Repeat with the remaining marked square and unit from step 1 to yield four flying-geese units. Trim the tails from the units. Make 96 units measuring 4½" × 8½", including seam allowances.

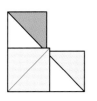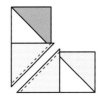

Make 96 units,
4½" × 8½".

CLIP THOSE THREADS

When chain stitching units that have a ¼" seam allowance on both sides of the drawn line, it's tempting to stitch everything on the right side of the drawn line and then flip the connected units around and stitch on the other side of the marked lines. However, the added weight of the chain pieces dangling in front of the machine often makes seam allowances less accurate. So, take an extra minute to clip the threads between your units before stitching on the second side of the drawn line. It can make a big difference in accuracy.

4 Lay out two units from step 3 and two flying-geese units in two rows as shown. Sew the units into rows and then join the rows. Make 16 Dutch Days blocks measuring 16½" square, including seam allowances.

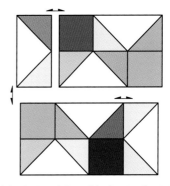

Make 16 Dutch Days blocks, 16½" × 16½".

BALANCING THE LAYOUT

Balancing the colors in the layout is important. Once you have an arrangement you like, snap a picture of the blocks and then view it on your computer or phone. Seeing the entire quilt as a small image without moving your eyes, you can easily tell if your colors are balanced or if you want to do a little rearranging.

3 Join two flying-geese units and two B squares as shown. Make 32 units measuring 8½" × 12½", including seam allowances.

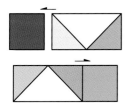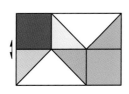

Make 32 units,
8½" × 12½".

If you find you really don't like cutting 4⅞" pieces, you can always upsize your pieces for the flying-geese units. Instead of 9¼" squares, cut 9½" squares and replace all of the 4⅞" squares with 5" squares. However, if you piece with these larger squares, you'll have to trim the completed units to 4½" x 8½". I highly recommend using a flying-geese trimming ruler (such as a 4½" x 8½" Bloc Loc ruler) for trimming the units to size. Otherwise, it can be tricky to ensure you maintain a ¼" seam allowance on all sides of the units.

assembling the quilt top

1 Join four blocks and five white 2" × 16½" strips to make a row. Make four rows measuring 16½" × 72", including seam allowances.

2 Join the 10 white 2" × 42" strips end to end in pairs. Trim each of the five pieced strips to 72" long for sashing.

3 Referring to the quilt assembly diagram below, join the sashing strips alternately with the block rows. The quilt top should measure 72" square.

finishing the quilt

1 Layer the quilt top with batting and backing; baste the layers together.

2 Quilt by hand or machine. The quilt shown is machine quilted with an echoed wavy orange peel design in the blocks. A curly line is stitched in the background.

3 Use the plum 2½"-wide strips to make double-fold binding. Attach the binding to the quilt.

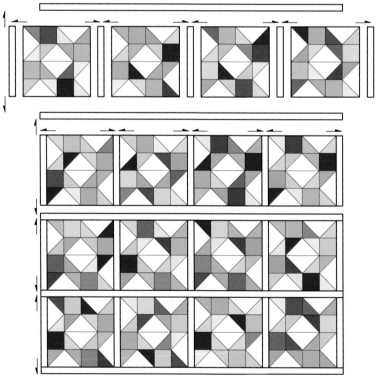

Quilt assembly

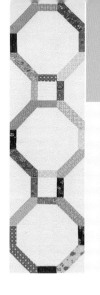

merry-go-round

It's so fun to play with interlocking units when designing quilts. Here I experimented with no-waste lattice units to create a honeycomb effect. When the quilt was finished, it was so bright and happy it felt more like a playground than a honeycomb; thus, the name Merry-Go-Round. Oh, and if you've never made no-waste lattice units before, you're going to have fun making this quilt!

materials

Yardage is based on 42"-wide fabric. A Riley Blake Designs 10" Stacker contains 42 squares, 10" × 10". Fabrics are Indigo Garden by Heather Peterson for Riley Blake Designs.

41 squares, 10" × 10", of assorted prints for blocks and binding

4⅞ yards of white solid for blocks and sashing

7 yards of fabric for backing (or 4¾ yards if fabric is at least 42" wide after washing and trimming selvages)

83" × 83" piece of batting

6½" × 6½" ruler

Washi tape

PLAN AHEAD

Divide the 10" squares into two groups as follows, and keep the fabrics labeled while making the blocks to achieve the desired results.

* *GROUP A: 26 assorted squares for blocks and binding*

* *GROUP B: 15 assorted squares for blocks and binding*

cutting

All measurements include ¼" seam allowances. Before you begin cutting, see "Plan Ahead," above.

From *each* of the A squares, cut:
3 strips, 2½" × 10" (78 total)
2 pieces, 2" × 4½" (52 total)

From *each* of the B squares, cut:
2 strips, 2½" × 10" (30 total)
4 pieces, 2" × 4½" (60 total)

From the white solid, cut:
11 strips, 5¾" × 42"; crosscut into 64 squares, 5¾" × 5¾".
  Cut the squares in half diagonally to yield 128 triangles.
21 strips, 4½" × 42"; crosscut into:
    24 strips, 4½" × 13½"
    64 pieces, 4½" × 5"
    25 squares, 4½" × 4½"

making the merry-go-round blocks

Press seam allowances in the directions indicated by the arrows.

1 Join one A or B 2" × 4½" piece and one white 4½" × 5" piece as shown. Make 64 side units measuring 4½" × 6½", including seam allowances.

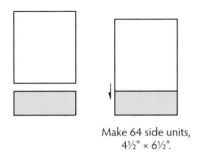

Make 64 side units,
4½" × 6½".

2 Center and sew a white triangle to an A or B strip. (See "Lattice Short Cuts" at right.) Center and sew a second white triangle on the opposite side of the strip. Make 64 lattice units. You'll have 44 A and B strips left over to use for the binding.

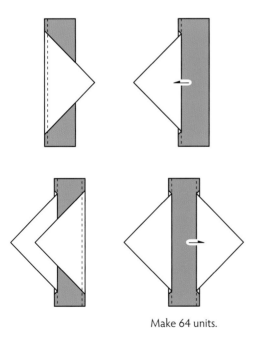

Make 64 units.

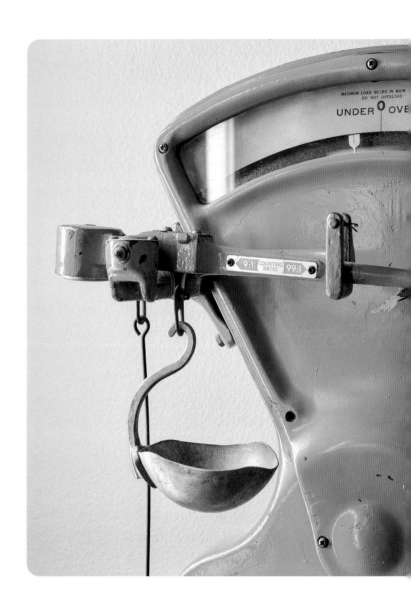

LATTICE SHORT CUTS

The instructions for the lattice units say to center the triangle on the A or B strip. You don't have to find the exact center. The units are oversized and will be trimmed, so simply eyeballing the center works great.

In addition, when sewing the ¼" seam allowance, it's faster to stitch along the entire length of the strip, even though it means you'll only sew on one piece of fabric at the top and bottom. It's still quicker to chain stitch the whole strip than to start and stop at the triangle.

3 Place a 6½" square ruler on top of the pattern on page 45. Use washi tape to mark the diagonal lines on the top of the ruler. Place the marked ruler on a lattice unit, aligning the marked diagonal lines with the seamlines. Trim along the four edges of the square ruler (see "Trimming" below). Make 64 lattice units measuring 6½" square, including seam allowances.

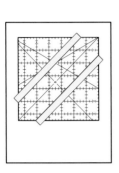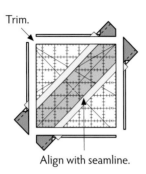

Trim.

Align with seamline.

Make 64 lattice units,
6½" × 6½".

TRIMMING

I recommend using the pattern on page 45 to mark your ruler so that each lattice unit is perfectly centered, making it easy to line up the blocks. I find the best tool for marking my rulers is washi tape. The tape sticks great but leaves no residue behind when removed.

And having the right ruler size for trimming makes all the difference. It's so much easier to trim all four sides at once than to trim just two and have to rotate the unit and realign the ruler. A 6½" square ruler is my go-to size, so if you don't have one, making this quilt is a great reason to get one. A rotating mat makes it super easy to trim all four sides without having to move the ruler.

ALIGNING THE ANGLED SEAMS

When you're joining the units to make the block, the angled seam on the bias will want to move inward on you. You can fix this and ensure that the points meet by making a mark ¼" from the outer edge on the wrong side of each unit. Use a positioning pin as described in "Perfect Points" on page 29 to match the two marks. Pin and then sew a ¼" seam allowance.

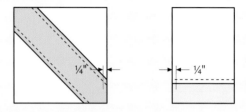

¼"   ¼"

4 Lay out four lattice units, four side units, and one white 4½" square in three rows, rotating the units as shown. Sew all the pieces into rows and then join the rows. Make 16 Merry-Go-Round blocks measuring 16½" square, including seam allowances.

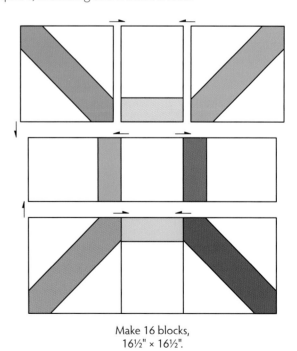

Make 16 blocks,
16½" × 16½".

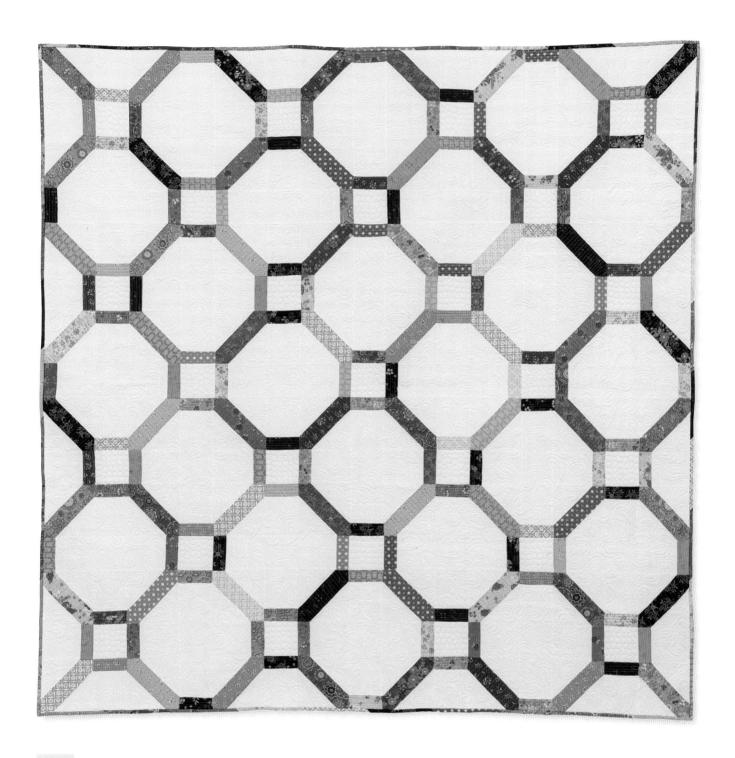

FINISHED QUILT: 76½" × 76½"
FINISHED BLOCKS: 16" × 16"

assembling the quilt top

Refer to the quilt assembly diagram below as needed throughout.

1 Join two A or B 2" × 4½" pieces and one white 4½" × 13½" strip to make a sashing unit. Make 24 units measuring 4½" × 16½", including seam allowances.

Make 24 units,
4½" × 16½".

2 Join four blocks and three sashing units to make a block row. Make four rows measuring 16½" × 76½", including seam allowances.

3 Join four sashing units and three white 4½" squares to make a sashing row. Make three rows measuring 4½" × 76½", including seam allowances.

4 Join the block rows alternately with the sashing rows. The quilt top should measure 76½" square.

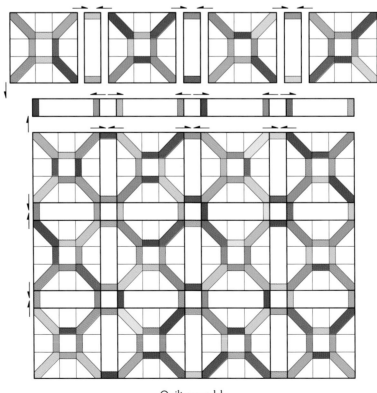

Quilt assembly

finishing the quilt

1 Stitch around the perimeter of the quilt top, ⅛" from the outer edges, to lock the seams in place.

2 Layer the quilt top with batting and backing; baste the layers together.

3 Quilt by hand or machine. The quilt shown is machine quilted with straight lines and pebbles in the blocks. Curlicues are stitched in the background.

4 Use the remaining A and B 2½" × 10" strips to make scrappy double-fold binding (see "Scrappy Bindings" on page 24). Attach the binding to the quilt.

Trimming template

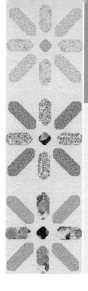

jacks

When I was a child, whenever we had recess indoors at school I always wanted to play jacks. It was the best. Designing this quilt brought back many fun memories of playing my favorite game. I hope it will for you as well. Jacks is made of a lot of tiny stitch-and-flip squares, but don't be overwhelmed. They're fast to finish with chain piecing, and the result is a great quilt to snuggle up in.

materials

Yardage is based on 42"-wide fabric. A Moda Fabrics Layer Cake contains 42 squares, 10" × 10". Fabrics are Paisley Rose by Crystal Manning for Moda Fabrics.

40 squares, 10" × 10", of assorted prints for blocks and binding

4½ yards of white solid for blocks and sashing

4¾ yards of fabric for backing

69" × 84" piece of batting

PLAN AHEAD

Divide the 10" squares into two groups as follows, and keep the fabrics labeled while making the blocks to achieve the desired results.

* *GROUP A: 20 assorted squares for blocks*

* *GROUP B: 20 assorted squares for blocks and binding*

cutting

All measurements include ¼" seam allowances. Before you begin cutting, see "Plan Ahead," below left.

From *each* of the A squares, cut:
4 strips, 2½" × 6½" (80 total)
2 squares, 2½" × 2½" (40 total; 8 are extra)

From *each* of the B squares, cut:
2 strips, 2½" × 10" (40 total; 3 are extra)
4 strips, 2½" × 5" (80 total)

From the white solid, cut:
10 strips, 5" × 42"; crosscut into 80 squares, 5" × 5". Cut the squares in half diagonally to yield 160 large triangles.
23 strips, 2½" × 42"; crosscut *16 of the strips* into:
     31 strips, 2½" × 13½"
     80 pieces, 1½" × 2½"
5 strips, 2¼" × 42"; crosscut into 80 squares, 2¼" × 2¼". Cut the squares in half diagonally to yield 160 small triangles.
24 strips, 1¼" × 42"; crosscut into 768 squares, 1¼" × 1¼"

SPEED UP THE CUTTING

I know, 768 squares is a lot to cut. To speed things up, use your mat for aligning and be sure you have a sharp rotary blade. Fold the fabric so you are cutting through four fabric layers at a time instead of just two. Cut 12 strips that are 1¼" wide, as you normally would. But since you're cutting through a double thickness of fabric, you'll actually be cutting 24 strips. Then without moving or rearranging the strips on your mat, align the ruler and crosscut the strips into 1¼" squares. Cut 16 squares from each stack of two folded strips. Just like that, you'll have all the squares you need! I use this method to cut out the background fabrics for all of my quilts.

FINISHED QUILT: 62½" × 77½"
FINISHED BLOCKS: 13" × 13"

making the jacks blocks

Press seam allowances in the directions indicated by the arrows.

1 Draw a diagonal line from corner to corner on the wrong side of the white 1¼" squares. Place marked squares on the corners of an A strip, right sides together. Sew on the marked lines. Trim the excess corner fabric ¼" from the stitched lines. Make 20 sets of four matching units measuring 2½" × 6½", including seam allowances. Set aside the remaining marked squares for later use.

 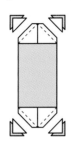 

Make 20 sets of
4 matching units,
2½" × 6½".

2 Fold two large white triangles in half and finger-press to mark the center of the long side. Fold a unit from step 1 in half and finger-press to mark the center on each long side. Sew the large triangles to opposite sides of the unit, aligning the center creases. Sew small white triangles to the short ends of the unit. Make 20 sets of four matching corner units and trim them to 6" square, including seam allowances.

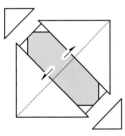 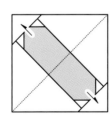

Make 20 sets of
4 matching units,
6" × 6".

SKIP THE LINE

Don't like drawing the line on all of those tiny squares? Instead of drawing lines, you can use any number of diagonal sewing-guide tools on your machine. See "Skip Drawing the Line" on page 28 for my personal favorites.

3 Place marked squares from step 1 on the corners of a B 2½" × 5" strip, right sides together. Sew on the marked lines. Trim the excess corner fabric ¼" from the stitched lines. Make 20 sets of four matching units measuring 2½" × 5", including seam allowances.

 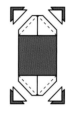 

Make 20 sets of
4 matching units,
2½" × 5".

4 Sew a white 1½" × 2½" piece to the bottom of each unit from step 3. Make 20 sets of four matching side units measuring 2½" × 6", including seam allowances.

Make 20 sets of
4 matching units,
2½" × 6".

SQUARING UP

You are mainly trimming the tails and then evening out the edges on the corner units (step 2, above). The nice thing is that because of those stitch-and-flip corners, this unit basically floats in the background, so don't stress too much about centering. As long as the units are 6" square, they will work.

5 Place the marked squares from step 1 on the corners of an A square, right sides together. Sew on the marked lines. Trim the excess corner fabric ¼" from the stitched lines. Make 32 square-in-a-square units.

Make 32 units, 2½" × 2½".

6 Lay out four matching corner units, four matching side units, and one square-in-a-square unit in three rows as shown. Sew the units into rows and then join the rows. Make 20 Jacks blocks measuring 13½" square, including seam allowances. Set aside the remaining square-in-a-square units for assembling the quilt top.

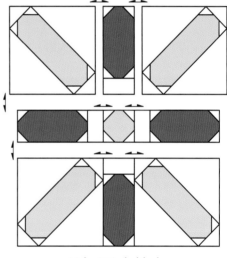

Make 20 Jacks blocks, 13½" × 13½".

assembling the quilt top

1 Referring to the quilt assembly diagram on page 51, join four blocks and three white 2½" × 13½" strips to make a block row. Make five rows measuring 13½" × 58½", including seam allowances.

2 Join four white 2½" × 13½" strips and three square-in-a-square units to make a sashing row. Make four rows measuring 2½" × 58½", including seam allowances.

3 Join the block rows alternately with the sashing rows. The quilt top should measure 58½" × 73½", including seam allowances.

4 Join the white 2½" × 42" strips end to end. From the pieced strip, cut two 73½"-long strips and two 62½"-long strips. Sew the longer strips to the left and right edges of the quilt top. Sew the shorter strips to the top and bottom edges. Press all seam allowances toward the white strips. The quilt top should measure 62½" × 77½".

Finishing the Quilt

1 Layer the quilt top with batting and backing; baste the layers together.

2 Quilt by hand or machine. The quilt shown is machine quilted with figure eights in the blocks. Loops and pebbles are stitched in the background.

3 Use the B 2½" × 10" strips to make scrappy double-fold binding (see "Scrappy Bindings" on page 24). Attach the binding to the quilt.

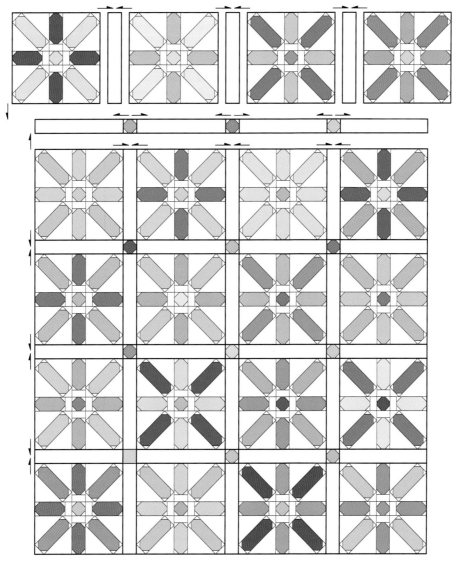

Quilt assembly

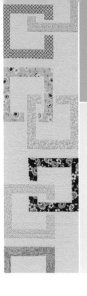

puzzle box

Puzzle Box is a fantastic interlocking geometric design that keeps your eyes moving. It was inspired by small metal brain puzzles that my kids were obsessed with while we were camping. The quilt looks a little complex, but with basic piecing it's a snap. Puzzle Box makes for a modern finish that's perfect for any occasion. And just in case you need to make a quilt for a man cave, this design is a good choice for a more masculine quilt.

materials

Yardage is based on 42"-wide fabric. A Moda Fabrics Layer Cake contains 42 squares, 10" × 10". Fabrics are Morning Light by Linzee Kull McCray for Moda Fabrics.

33 squares, 10" × 10", of assorted prints for blocks and binding

2¾ yards of white solid for blocks and sashing

3⅞ yards of fabric for backing

68" × 68" piece of batting

PLAN AHEAD

When choosing the A and B fabrics, decide which two fabrics to combine for each block, going for as much contrast as you can when picking the A and B fabrics. Match large-scale busy prints with small-scale prints. Contrasting light and dark prints will make your blocks stand out.

Divide the 10" squares into three groups as follows, and keep the fabrics labeled while making the blocks to achieve the desired results.

✳ *GROUP A: 16 assorted squares for blocks and binding*

✳ *GROUP B: 16 assorted squares for blocks and binding*

✳ *GROUP C: 1 square for binding*

cutting

All measurements include ¼" seam allowances. Before you begin cutting, see "Plan Ahead," below left. As you cut, keep like fabrics together.

From *each* of the A and B squares, cut:
1 strip, 2½" × 10" (32 total)
5 strips, 2" × 7½"; crosscut into:
    1 strip, 2" × 6½" (32 total)
    3 strips, 2" × 5" (96 total)
    1 piece, 2" × 4½" (32 total)
    1 piece, 2" × 3" (32 total)
    1 square, 2" × 2" (32 total)

From the C square, cut:
4 strips, 2½" × 10"

From the white solid, cut:
4 strips, 5" × 42"; crosscut into 32 squares, 5" × 5"
9 strips, 3½" × 42"; crosscut into:
    32 strips, 3½" × 6½"
    32 squares, 3½" × 3½"
19 strips, 2" × 42"; crosscut *11 of the strips* into:
    20 strips, 2" × 14"
    16 squares, 2" × 2"
    64 pieces, 1" × 2"

BACKGROUND FABRIC

This design has a large amount negative space. Don't be afraid to pick something other than a solid to fill that negative space and add a little punch to your quilt.

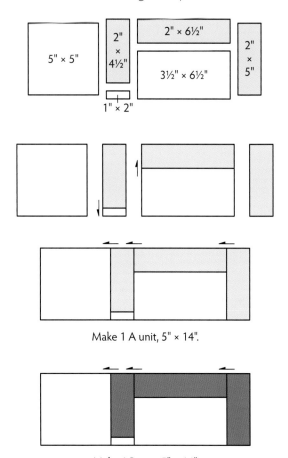

Make 1 A unit, 5" × 14".

Make 1 B unit, 5" × 14".

making the puzzle box blocks

For each block, select the following pieces.

From 1 A and 1 B print:

1 piece, 2" × 4½" (2 total)

1 strip, 2" × 6½" (2 total)

3 strips, 2" × 5" (6 total)

1 piece, 2" × 3" (2 total)

1 square, 2" × 2" (2 total)

From the white solid:

2 squares, 5" × 5"

2 strips, 3½" × 6½"

2 squares, 3½" × 3½"

4 pieces, 1" × 2"

1 square, 2" × 2"

The instructions are for making one block; repeat to make 16 blocks. Press seam allowances in the directions indicated by the arrows.

1 Using matching pieces from the A print, lay out one 2" × 4½" piece, one 2" × 6½" strip, and one 2" × 5" strip, along with one white 5" square, one white 1" × 2" piece, and one white 3½" × 6½" strip as shown. Sew the pieces into columns and then join the columns. Add

2 Join an A 2" × 3" and a white 1" × 2" piece. Sew a white 3½" square to the left edge to make a unit measuring 5" × 3½", including seam allowances. Make a second unit using the B pieces.

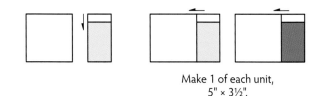

Make 1 of each unit, 5" × 3½".

3 Lay out the two units from step 2, one white 2" square, A and B 2" squares, and A and B 2" × 5" strips. Sew the pieces into columns. Join the columns and then add the A and B 2" × 5" strips to make a unit measuring 5" × 14", including seam allowances.

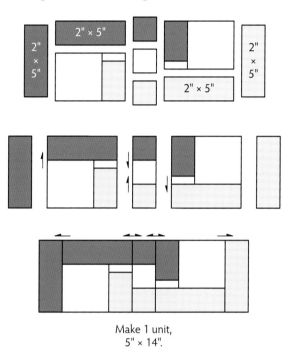

Make 1 unit,
5" × 14".

4 Lay out the two units from step 1 and the unit from step 3 as shown. Join the units to make a block. Repeat to make 16 Puzzle Box blocks measuring 14" square, including seam allowances.

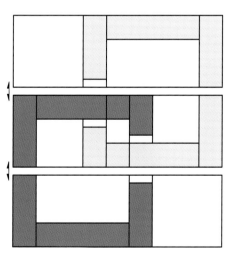

Make 16 blocks,
14" × 14".

FINISHED QUILT: 62" × 62"
FINISHED BLOCKS: 13½" × 13½"

assembling the quilt top

1 Referring to the quilt assembly diagram below, join five white 2" × 14" strips and four blocks to make a block row. Make four rows measuring 14" × 62", including seam allowances.

2 Join the white 2" × 42" strips end to end. From the pieced strip, cut five 62"-long sashing strips.

3 Join the block rows alternately with the 62"-long sashing strips (see "Sewing Sashing Straight" on page 63). The quilt top should measure 62" square.

finishing the quilt

1 Stitch around the perimeter of the quilt top, ⅛" from the outer edges, to lock the seams in place.

2 Layer the quilt top with batting and backing; baste the layers together.

3 Quilt by hand or machine. The quilt shown is machine quilted with straight lines in the blocks and meandering boxes in the background.

4 Use the A, B, and C 2½" × 10" strips to make scrappy double-fold binding (see "Scrappy Bindings" on page 24). Attach the binding to the quilt.

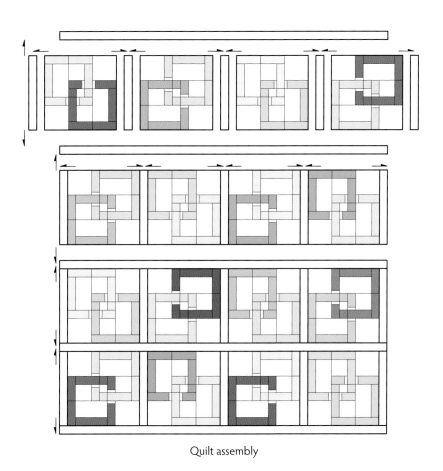

Quilt assembly

treasured

When I first designed this quilt, I called it X Marks the Spot. But when the quilt was finished, it was just way too pretty for that name. So what goes with X Marks the Spot? Obviously, it's where you find the treasure. Then it hit me: this would be a Treasured quilt for anyone! I hope it's truly a treasure for you or a loved one.

materials

Yardage is based on 42"-wide fabric. A Riley Blake Design 10" Stacker contains 42 squares, 10" × 10". Fabrics are Sonnet Dusk by Corri Sheff for Riley Blake Designs.

39 squares, 10" × 10", of assorted prints for blocks and binding

3 yards of white solid for blocks and sashing

3⅜ yards of fabric for backing

59" × 75" piece of batting

PLAN AHEAD

If you happen to be using a precut bundle of squares that has a lot of repeat prints in it, I highly recommend using the repeats in different fabric groups. This will give your quilt a scrappier look and avoid using the same print in the same spot from one block to the next.

Divide the 10" squares into four groups as follows, and keep the fabrics labeled while making the blocks to achieve the desired results.

❋ *GROUP A: 12 assorted squares for blocks and binding*

❋ *GROUP B: 12 assorted squares for side units and binding*

❋ *GROUP C: 12 assorted squares for side and center units*

❋ *GROUP D: 3 assorted squares for binding*

cutting

All measurements include ¼" seam allowances. Before you begin cutting, see "Plan Ahead," below left.

From *each* of the A squares, cut:
4 squares, 3½" × 3½" (48 total)
1 strip, 2½" × 10" (12 total)

From *each* of the B squares, cut:
2 strips, 3½" × 10"; crosscut into 8 pieces, 2" × 3½" (96 total)
1 strip, 2½" × 10" (12 total)

From *each* of the C squares, refer to the diagram below to cut:
4 squares, 3½" × 3½" (48 total)
8 squares, 2" × 2" (96 total)

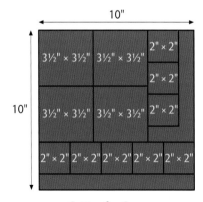

Cutting for C squares

From *each* of the D squares, cut:
4 strips, 2½" × 10" (12 total)

continued on page 60

continued from page 58

From the white solid, cut:

13 strips, 4½" × 42"; crosscut *6 of the strips* into 16 strips, 4½" × 12½"

5 strips, 3½" × 42"; crosscut into 48 squares, 3½" × 3½"

10 strips, 2" × 42"; crosscut into 192 squares, 2" × 2"

making the treasured blocks

Press seam allowances in the directions indicated by the arrows.

1 Draw a diagonal line from corner to corner on the wrong side of the white 2" squares. Place a marked square on the end of a B 2" × 3½" piece, right sides together. Sew on the marked line. Trim the excess corner fabric ¼" from the stitched line. Make 48 left units measuring 2" × 3½", including seam allowances. In the same way, use the remaining B pieces and marked squares to make 48 right units, noting the direction of the marked line. You should have 48 sets, with each set consisting of one left unit and one right unit from the same print. You'll have 96 marked squares to use in step 2.

Make 48 of each unit, 2" × 3½".

NO MARKING

I really don't like drawing lots of lines. You can skip drawing lines by using any number of diagonal marking tools on your machine. See "Skip Drawing the Line" on page 28 for my favorite time-saving tools!

2 Place a marked square from step 1 on one corner of a C 3½" square, right sides together. Sew on the marked line. Trim the excess corner fabric ¼" from the stitched line. Place a marked square on an adjacent corner. Sew and trim as before to make a unit measuring 3½" square, including seam allowances. Repeat to make 48 units.

Make 48 units, 3½" × 3½".

3 Join one left unit, one unit from step 2, and one matching right unit. Make 12 sets of four matching side units measuring 3½" × 6½", including seam allowances.

 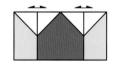

Make 12 sets of 4 units, 3½" × 6½".

4 Draw a diagonal line from corner to corner on the wrong side of the C 2" squares. Place marked squares on opposite corners of a white 3½" square, right sides together. Sew on the marked lines. Trim the excess corner fabric ¼" from the stitched lines. Make 12 sets of four matching units measuring 3½" square, including seam allowances.

Make 12 sets of 4 matching units, 3½" × 3½".

5 Lay out four matching units from step 4 in two rows, rotating the units as shown. Sew the units into rows and then join the rows. Make 12 center units measuring 6½" square, including seam allowances.

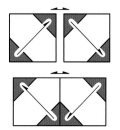
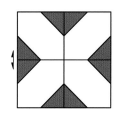

Make 12 center units,
6½" × 6½".

PERFECT POINTS

When piecing the blocks, you'll have a lot of points to line up. For help, see "Aligning the Angled Seams" on page 42.

see "Aligning the Angled Seams" on page 42.

6 Lay out four matching A squares, four matching side units, and one matching center unit in three rows as shown. Sew all the pieces into rows and then join the rows to make a block. Make 12 Treasured blocks measuring 12½" square, including seam allowances.

PRESS FOR SUCCESS

Pressing the seam allowances in the indicated directions will allow the diagonal seams to nest, which makes it much easier to join units and blocks accurately. When pressing the seam allowances in the same direction within a unit from step 4, press the unit from the right side. When laying out the center unit, take care to position the pressed seam allowances in opposite directions from one unit to the next, so the seams will nest.

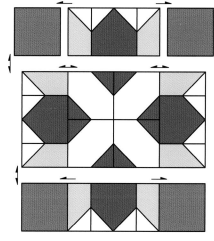

Make 12 blocks,
12½" × 12½".

FINISHED QUILT: 52½" × 68½"
FINISHED BLOCKS: 12" × 12"

assembling the quilt top

1 Referring to the quilt assembly diagram below, join four white 4½" × 12½" strips and three blocks to make a block row. Make four rows measuring 12½" × 52½", including seam allowances.

2 Join the 4½" × 42" strips end to end. From the pieced strip, cut five 52½"-long sashing strips.

3 Join the 52½"-long sashing strips alternately with the block rows. The quilt top should measure 52½" × 68½".

SEWING SASHING STRAIGHT

It's very noticeable when blocks and vertical sashing strips aren't lined up on both sides of long horizontal sashing strips. An easy way to align them is to pin the long sashing strips at the junctions that must match. Mark off the width for each vertical sashing strip and each pieced block, and then join the rows.

finishing the quilt

1 Stitch around the perimeter of the quilt top, ⅛" from the outer edges, to lock the seams in place.

2 Layer the quilt top with batting and backing; baste the layers together.

3 Quilt by hand or machine. The quilt shown is machine quilted with straight lines, arches, figure eights, and pebbles in the blocks. Feathered swirls are stitched in the background.

4 Use the A, B, and D 2½" × 10" strips to make scrappy double-fold binding (see "Scrappy Bindings" on page 24). Attach the binding to the quilt.

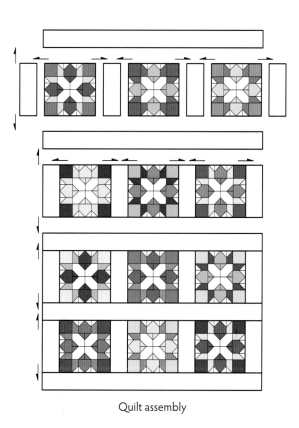

Quilt assembly

HELPFUL RESOURCES

Some of the processes described in this book may be unfamiliar to you, especially if you're new to quilting. If you'd like more information on any of them, I invite you to visit my blog, where you can find several video and picture tutorials. I hope these pointers help you learn new techniques and aid you along your quilting journey. You can find me online at: HappyQuiltingMelissa.com

ACKNOWLEDGMENTS

I'm so grateful for the help and support of family and friends during the making of this book! Special thanks go to:

My family members—Jacob, Spencer, Jessica, Kristian, Kamryn, and Jocelyn. Thank you for your patience, support, encouragement, and love.

My amazing mother-in-law, Barbara. Thank you for your countless hours spent hand binding each and every quilt in this book, for letting me take over the long-arm machine, and for always being there to offer advice, help in a pinch, and give encouragement along every step of the way.

My mother, Christine. Thank you for starting this love of quilting within me, and for being my sounding board and having endless phone chats over design, color, and second thoughts. And thank you for always believing in me.

My twin sister, Jennifer. Thank you for always being on the other end of FaceTime, and for helping me come up with quilt names when I'm at a complete loss. And thank you for always encouraging me.

Moda Fabrics. Thank you for providing the beautiful fabrics featured in Aurora, Diamond Dash, Jacks, Keystone Corners, Puzzle Box, and Three in a Row. And thank you to so many individual wonderful friends at Moda who always reach out, support, and help me grow as a quilter.

Riley Blake Designs. Thank you for providing the beautiful fabrics featured in Dutch Days, Merry-Go-Round, and Treasured, and for allowing me to be a part of your fabric blog tours and Garden of Quilts.

My wonderful Happy Quilting readers. Thank you for your daily encouragement. Your comments, emails, and pictures mean the world to me and are a constant reminder of why I love this industry and the amazing people in it.

about the author

Melissa began quilting as a hobby in 2005, but since starting her Happy Quilting blog in 2010 her hobby has turned into a passion. Her enthusiasm for quilting has led to creating her own designs that she shares as tutorials, published works, a pattern line, and even her own books, including *Irish Chain Quilts* and now *Fast & Fun Lap Quilts*. Melissa finds design inspiration in just about anything and everything. Melissa, her husband, and their five children live in Cedar City, Utah. To enjoy more of her daily quilting adventures, check out her blog at HappyQuiltingMelissa.com.